A Cheer for Me!

I can read a book.
I can learn to cook.
I can count to 103.

I can walk with a wiggle
That makes you giggle
Or buzz like a bumblebee.

It will always be true
That I am not just like you,
But I make a wonderful me!

◆ **Underline the right answers.**

1. What is another good name for the poem?

   I'm the Best Me!   I Am Better Than You

2. Which word rhymes with **giggle**?

   make   wiggle   bumblebee

3. What does **wonderful** mean?

   bad   really great   silly

◆ **Unscramble the word to answer the question.**

4. What does a bumblebee do?

   _____

   zubz _____

What Is Missing?

◆ Draw what is missing in each picture.

1.

2.

3.

4.

5.

6.

2

Making Inferences/Cause and Effect

Bone Mystery

Dog likes to make things. When he works, Dog often does things without thinking.

Yesterday Dog made a table. When the table was done, he wanted to chew on a big bone. But his four bones were gone! Can you find Dog's bones?

◆ **Underline the right answers.**

1. What is the best name for the story?

   My Bones Are Missing!   Dog Works Hard

2. What does Dog often forget to do?

   play   think   chew

3. What happened to Dog's bones?

   They were stolen.   They were thrown out.   Dog used them.

4. What does "do things without thinking" mean?

   not think about what you do   chew on a nice big bone

5. Which thing was named in the story?

Main Idea/Drawing Conclusions

Make a Book

You can make a book.
You need paper, a pencil,
crayons, and a stapler.

Stack some paper.
Staple along the side.
Draw a cover. Write a
story. Draw pictures, too.

◆ **What are two things you need to make a book?**

1. _____   _____

◆ **Put the steps in order. Write 1, 2, 3, 4, and 5.**

2. ☐ Staple along the side.   ☐ Stack some paper.   ☐ Draw a cover.

☐ Draw pictures inside.   ☐ Write a story.

Selecting Details/Steps in a Process

Mouse TV

Five white mice were on TV.
They had a show on Channel 3.

The first white mouse played a rat-ta-tat-tum.
The second white mouse began to hum.

The third white mouse tap-tapped his feet.
The fourth white mouse clapped out the beat.

The fifth white mouse sang about a cat.
Mouse TV—imagine that!

◆ Draw lines to show what the mice did.

hummed along

danced around

played a drum

sang a song

clapped his hands

Selecting Details/Sequence of Events

What's Next?

◆ **Underline what happens next.**

1. Mick loves movies. He goes every time he has money. Mick got $5.00 from his uncle. What happens next?

2. PJ's mom gave her flower seeds. PJ made a garden. She planted the seeds every which way. What happens next?

3. Jerry forgets things. He took some books to show Andy. The kids were playing tag. Jerry played too. It was time to go home. What happens next?

4. Mia's pup chewed her homework. He chewed a chair leg. Now he lives outside. Mia left her shoes in the yard. What happens next?

Drawing Conclusions/Predicting Outcomes

How Do You Use It?

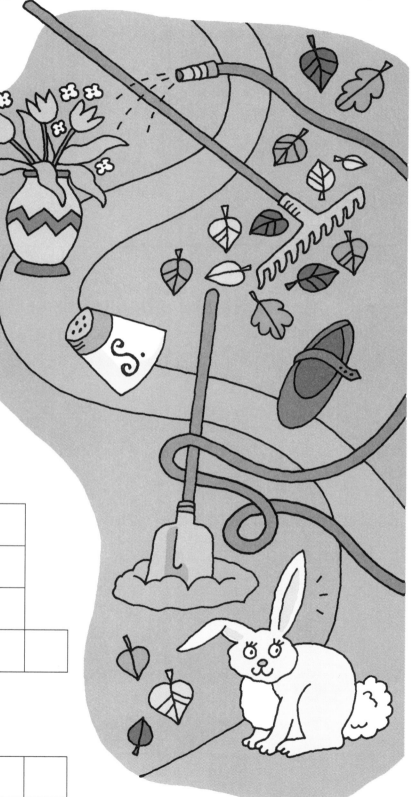

◆ **Read the clues. Write the words in the puzzle. Use these words if you need help.**

hose   path   shaker   shoe
shovel   rake   vase   ear

Across ▶

1. Use it to pour salt.

3. Use it to dig.

5. Use it to walk in the woods.

6. Use it to put out fires.

7. Use it to listen.

Down ▼

2. Use it to pile leaves.

3. Use it to cover your foot.

4. Use it for flowers.

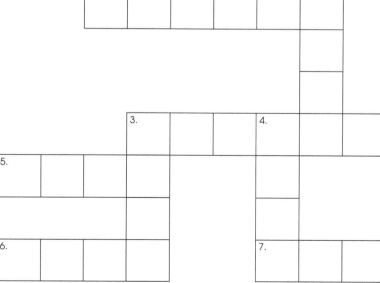

A Letter from Camp

Hi, Jon,   July 15

Camp is no fun. It rains every day! We can't go outside. We can't play baseball. There is no TV!

I'm glad I can read. I've read 10 books in 3 days. I read books all day. I use my flashlight to read at night. Send me more books. Hurry!

Your friend,
Jamie

◆ **Crack the code! Read each question.**
If the answer is yes, circle the letter under Yes.
If the answer is no, circle the letter under No.

	Yes	No
1. Does Jamie like camp?	O	T
2. Could Jamie watch TV?	L	H
3. Did it rain at camp?	E	D
4. Did Jamie have to stay inside?	R	B
5. Is Jamie a good reader?	A	O
6. Does Jamie want to play baseball?	I	O
7. Did Jamie lose her flashlight?	K	N

◆ **Write the circled letters in the boxes.**

8. What caused Jamie's problems?

			■				

Computer Cat

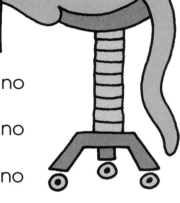

Computer Cat is a whiz on her computer. She can make drawings with her mouse. She can write long letters with the keys. She can write stories, too.

Computer Cat is writing a book. The book is about using a cat computer. She will sell her book on TV! Would you buy it?

◆ **Underline the right answers.**

1. What is the story about?

   a cat who uses a computer   a cat and a mouse

2. Does Computer Cat draw pictures?   yes   no

3. Does Computer Cat chase her mouse?   yes   no

4. Does Computer Cat write letters?   yes   no

5. Which cat is Computer Cat?

Main Idea/Supporting Details

Nightmare!

Henry was sleeping. He dreamed he was being chased through a jungle. A lion wanted to eat him! The lion was red. Then it was blue. Then it was yellow. But the lion's teeth were always white.

Finally Henry woke up. He was glad the dream was over!

◆ **Underline the right answers.**

1. What is another good name for the story?

   Henry's Dream   Make-Believe Lions

2. What did Henry dream about?

   a lion chasing him   rainbows in the sky   going to bed

3. Where were Henry and the lion?

   in bed   in the jungle   on a rainbow

4. What is a nightmare?

   a bad dream   a lion   teeth

◆ **Draw a line to the end of each sentence.**

5. The lion   were always white.

   The lion's teeth   was red.

   Finally Henry   woke up.

Main Idea/Supporting Details/Building Vocabulary

Make Up a Superhero

Have you seen superheroes on TV? Superheroes do things that real people cannot. Some superheroes can fly. Some can shoot lightning.

Make up a superhero. Give your superhero a name. Give him or her a special power. What costume will your superhero wear?

◆ Write about your superhero. Draw a picture of your superhero.

1. What is your superhero's name?
   _____
   - - - - - - - - - - - - - - - - -
   _____

2. What is your superhero's power?
   _____
   - - - - - - - - - - - - - - - - -
   _____
   - - - - - - - - - - - - - - - - -
   _____

3. What does your superhero wear?
   _____
   - - - - - - - - - - - - - - - - -
   _____
   - - - - - - - - - - - - - - - - -
   _____
   - - - - - - - - - - - - - - - - -
   _____

My Superhero

Elephants and People

Elephants are a lot like people. They can live to be 70 years old. They live together in families. They take care of each other. Elephants even take baths!

Elephants are different from people, though. Elephants sleep in the day and eat at night. A baby elephant might weigh 200 pounds. A grown-up elephant can be 11 feet tall.

◆ **Write the answers to finish the chart.**

QUESTIONS	ELEPHANTS	MOST PEOPLE
1. How do they live?	live in	live in families
2. How do they stay clean?	take	take baths and showers
3. When do they sleep?	sleep in the	sleep at night
4. How big are babies?	might weigh _____ pounds	might weigh 13 pounds

Squirmy Slime

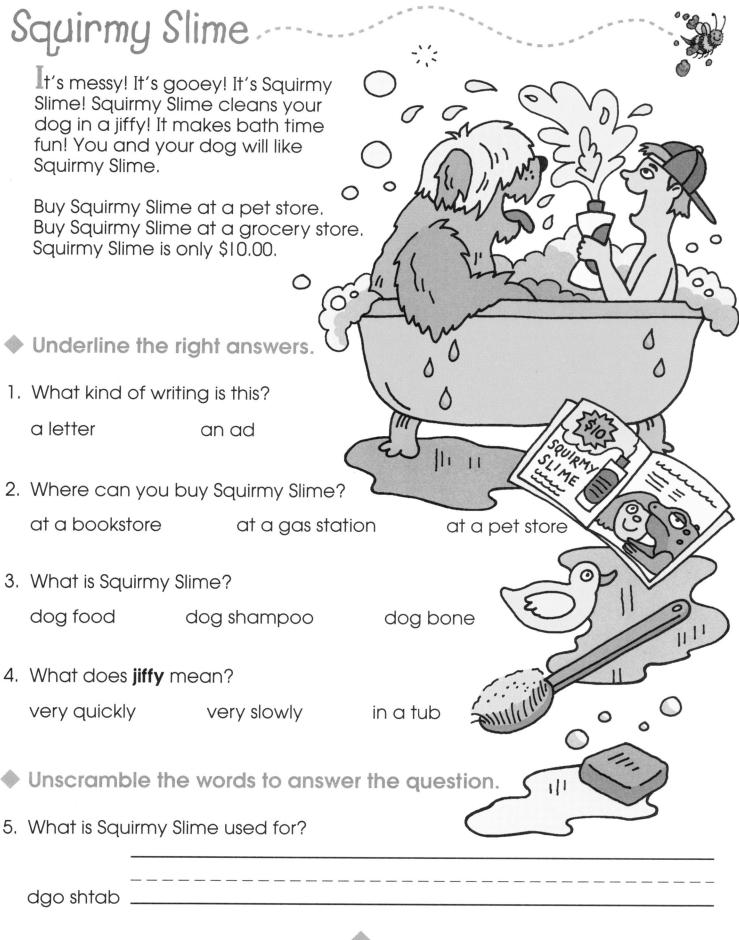

It's messy! It's gooey! It's Squirmy Slime! Squirmy Slime cleans your dog in a jiffy! It makes bath time fun! You and your dog will like Squirmy Slime.

Buy Squirmy Slime at a pet store. Buy Squirmy Slime at a grocery store. Squirmy Slime is only $10.00.

◆ **Underline the right answers.**

1. What kind of writing is this?

   a letter   an ad

2. Where can you buy Squirmy Slime?

   at a bookstore   at a gas station   at a pet store

3. What is Squirmy Slime?

   dog food   dog shampoo   dog bone

4. What does **jiffy** mean?

   very quickly   very slowly   in a tub

◆ **Unscramble the words to answer the question.**

5. What is Squirmy Slime used for?

   _____

   -

   dgo shtab _____

Scary Soup

Grandma was making soup for lunch. Eric told Andy that it was snake soup. He used the ladle to show her a snake. Andy did not like it one bit!

At lunch, Andy told Grandma she would not eat snakes! Grandma just laughed. "Oh, Andy!" she said. "They are just noodles!"

◆ **Underline the right answers.**

1. What is another good name for the story?

   Snake Soup   Eric's Dream   Grandma Frowns

2. What kind of soup was really in the pan?

   snake soup   tomato soup   noodle soup

3. How do you use a ladle?

   to scoop   to wash

4. What did Eric say was in the soup?

5. Who was cooking lunch?

Main Idea/Supporting Details/Building Vocabulary

Recycle

Jeff wants to recycle things. Sorting things to recycle them helps the earth.

Jeff must put things together. He must put the paper things together. He must put the cans together. He must put the plastic things together. Can you help Jeff recycle?

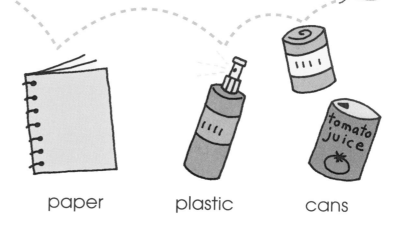

paper plastic cans

◆ **Draw lines to show where the objects go.**

Classifying/Using Context Clues

School Book Fair

Come to the Book Fair!

Bring books
you have read.
Trade for books
you want to read!

The Book Fair is in the school gym
Saturday, September 24.

Open All Day! Open All Day!

◆ **Underline the right answers.**

1. What kind of fair is it?   book fair   game fair

2. What should you bring?   books   money

3. What will you get there?   books   money

4. Where is the fair?   lunchroom   gym

5. When is the fair open?   all morning   all day

6. Why do you think the school has a book fair?

_____

_____

_____

_____

Selecting Details/Drawing Conclusions

Plant a Tree

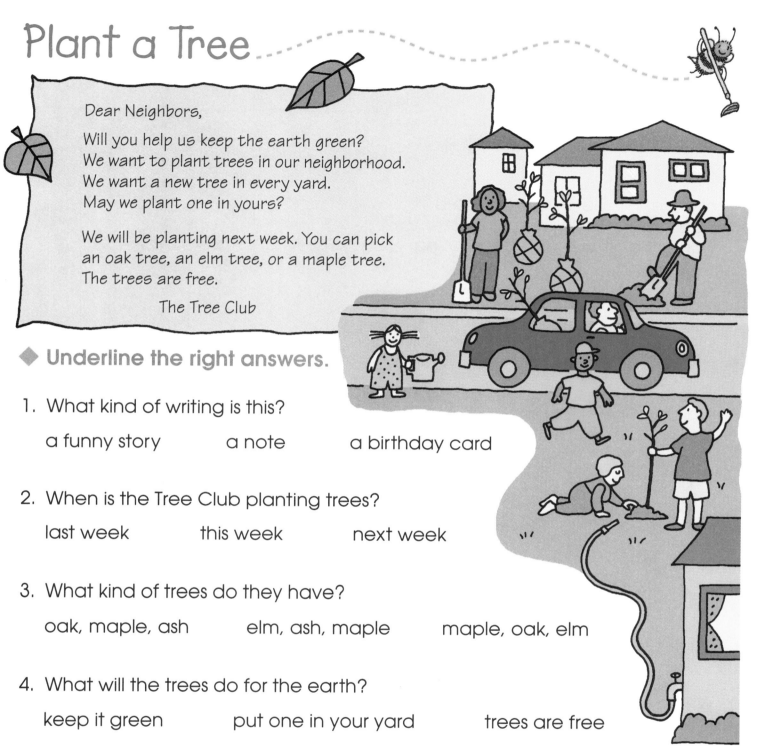

Dear Neighbors,

Will you help us keep the earth green?
We want to plant trees in our neighborhood.
We want a new tree in every yard.
May we plant one in yours?

We will be planting next week. You can pick
an oak tree, an elm tree, or a maple tree.
The trees are free.

The Tree Club

◆ **Underline the right answers.**

1. What kind of writing is this?

   a funny story   a note   a birthday card

2. When is the Tree Club planting trees?

   last week   this week   next week

3. What kind of trees do they have?

   oak, maple, ash   elm, ash, maple   maple, oak, elm

4. What will the trees do for the earth?

   keep it green   put one in your yard   trees are free

5. Which picture shows the Tree Club?

Identifying Genre/Supporting Details

Sport Fun!

Which sport is best? Miss Miller's class voted for a sport. Each child put up a sticker to show which sport is best.

There were four stickers from which to choose. Helmets were for football. Hats were for baseball. Fins were for swimming. Shoes were for running.

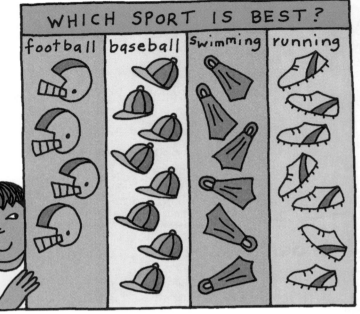

◆ **Underline the right answers.**

1. Which sticker is for running?

2. What does **voted** mean?

   chose the one you wanted   chose the one you didn't want

3. Which sport won in Miss Miller's class vote?

   football   baseball   running

◆ **Draw the sticker you would choose.**

Reward!

LOST DOG

He was last seen at
222 West Marble Street.

He has a white face
and a white tail.
His name is Spinner.

If you find him,
please call 555-7123.

REWARD!

◆ **Underline the right answers.**

1. What kind of writing is this?

   a birthday card   a sign   a newspaper

2. What is the sign for?

   to find a lost dog   to sell a dog   to give a dog a home

3. What does **reward** mean?

   a paper saying you are bad   something given for doing a good deed

4. Which dog is lost?

Betty Bunny

It was early morning. Betty Bunny awoke to a noise. Crash! Bang! Clang! Something was in her kitchen! She was frightened.

Could it be mice? Then Betty heard a creak on the stair. Slowly her door opened. It was the baby bunnies! They had cooked her breakfast.

◆ **Underline the right answers.**

1. What is a creak?

   water   animal   sound

2. When did this story happen?

   early morning   at lunchtime   late at night

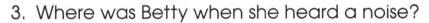

3. Where was Betty when she heard a noise?

  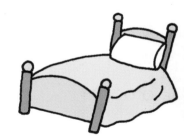

4. What did Betty think was making the noise?

Building Vocabulary/Selecting Details/Making Inferences

Save the Animals

The kids played a prank!
They hid the animals at the zoo.
They left a note. But the note is
written in code.

Read the note to find out how
many animals are missing.

◆ **Follow the directions to read the note.
Cross out the Cs, Ds, Js, and Qs.**

Dear Zookeepers: These are the animals we hid.																
T	D	W	Q	O	J	Z	E	B	R	A	S	Q	C	Q	J
Q	C	J	O	N	E	J	E	L	E	P	H	A	N	T	D
T	D	J	E	Q	Q	N	D	S	N	A	K	E	S	Q	J
C	D	O	J	C	N	Q	E	D	G	I	R	A	F	F	E
F	C	O	J	U	Q	R	J	M	O	N	K	E	Y	S	D

◆ **Draw your favorite missing animal.**

Play Flashlight Tag

Did you ever play flashlight tag? Flashlight tag is a little like tag and a little like hide-and-seek. All you need is a flashlight and some friends.

Here's how to play. Hold on to the flashlight. Have your friends hide. Try to find someone. Use the light to tag your friend. Give your friend the flashlight. Then start over.

◆ **What do you need to play?**

1. _____

◆ **Put the steps in order. Write 1, 2, 3, 4, 5, and 6.**

2. ☐ Find someone hiding.   ☐ Hold the flashlight.   ☐ Have friends hide.

☐ Give up the flashlight.   ☐ Tag someone hiding.   ☐ Go hide.

Match the Books

◆ Draw a line to match each book to its cover.

1.

The donkey carries things for people.

A Ride Long Ago

Trains go through the mountains.

Silly Animal Stories

Long ago there were no cars. People rode horses.

Real Working Animals

The elephant flew. The donkey flew.

Where Real Trains Go

◆ Underline the right answers.

2. Which books could be about real life?	1	2	3	4
3. Which books could not be about real life?	1	2	3	4
4. Which books would you like to read?	1	2	3	4

Real and Make-Believe/Background Knowledge

Make a Chart

◆ Write each word in the correct group.

Things People Play	Things People Wear	Things People Eat

Classifying/Using Picture Clues

A Fun Phone!

Make a simple telephone. You need two clean paper cups and a long piece of string.

Put a hole in the bottom of each cup. Push the string through the holes. Tie knots in the ends of the string inside of each cup.

Put one cup to your ear. Have a friend talk in the other cup. What do you hear?

◆ **Underline the right answers.**

1. What is another good name for the story?

   Two Fancy Cups   Make a Telephone

2. What can you make with two cups and some string?

   a telephone   a television   a telescope

3. Where do you put a hole?

   in the bottom of one cup   in the bottom of both cups

4. Where do you tie a knot?

   in one end of the string   in both ends of the string

◆ **What you would say to your friend on the telephone?**

5. _____

_____

_____

No Cookies!

Every day Bear came to my door. Every day he asked for a cookie. He did not want cake. He did not want ice cream. He just wanted cookies. I always said "Not today. Not ever. Bears do not eat cookies!"

One day Bear came to my door. He gave me a present. It was a giant bag of cookies. Bear said, "May I have a cookie, please?" I said, "Sure."

◆ **Underline the right answers.**

1. How often did Bear come?

   once a week   every day   one day

2. What did Bear bring one day?

   cookies   cake   ice cream

3. What does **giant** mean?

   very small   very old   very big

◆ **Write the word to finish each sentence.**

4. Every day, Bear came to my _____ .

5. "May I have a cookie, _____ ?"

Under the Sink

Julie ran into the yard. "Mom, come quick!" she said. "There is a snake under the sink!" Mom dropped the hose. She rushed in. There was a snake under the sink! She pushed it with a broom.

Alex ran in. "That's my toy snake," he laughed. Mom and Julie laughed, too.

◆ **Underline the right answers.**

1. What scared Julie?

2. Where did Julie find the snake?

   in the yard   under the sink   under her bed

3. What did Mom use to push the snake?

4. Why did Alex laugh?

   Mom was trying to help.   The snake was just a toy.

Free Tickets!

Dear Loni,

My dad got free tickets to the circus. Will you go with me? The tickets are for Sunday, June 9. The show starts at 3:00.

I cannot wait! I want to laugh at the clowns. The performers wear sparkling costumes. My dad said there is a man who is shot from a cannon!

Your very best friend,
Kate

◆ **Underline the right answers.**

1. Where does Kate want Loni to go?

   to the circus   to her house   shopping

2. What will Kate do when she sees the clowns?

   laugh   get free tickets   shoot a cannon

3. When will the show start?

   Sunday, June 3 at 9:00   Sunday, June 9 at 3:00

4. What is a performer?

   someone who puts on a show   someone who watches the circus

Supporting Details/Building Vocabulary

Make an Award

Marci makes her own special wrapping paper. She uses old newspapers and paints them with bright colors. Recycled paper doesn't use up trees. Marci's friend made her an award for taking care of the earth by recycling old newspapers.

Award

This award is given to

Marci

for

taking care of the earth.

◆ Make an award for someone you know.

Award

Animal Puzzle

◆ Read the clues. Write the words in the puzzle. Use these words if you need help.

anteater   bear   elephant   horse
panda   seal   snake   zebra   monkey

Across ▶

3. People can ride one.

4. Smokey is one.

7. Dumbo is one.

8. A teddy bear might be one.

9. This has no legs.

Down ▼

1. This is like a chimp.

2. This looks like a horse with stripes.

5. This eats bugs.

6. This swims, but isn't a fish.

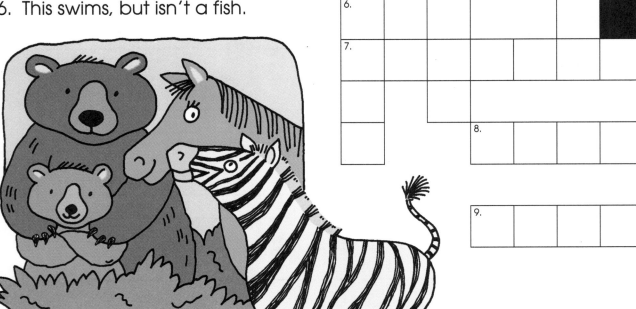

Following Directions/Making Inferences

What's Next?

◆ **Underline what happens next.**

1. Carlo turned on the water. He was going to do dishes. Carlo started talking to his friend. What happens next?

2. Cindy's mom went out. Cindy cleaned the house. Her mom came home. What happens next?

3. Eva went to the library. She picked out a book. She couldn't wait to read it. Eva took the book home. What happens next?

4. Frank's family lives near the woods. When it's cold, animals try to get in the house. Frank left the back door open. What happens next?

Cause and Effect/Making Predictions

Garden Groups

Gina is helping Dad clean the shed. Dad keeps the garden tools in groups.

Gina puts the watering tools on the left side of the shed. She puts the digging tools on the back wall. She puts the mowing tools outside the shed on the right.

◆ **Draw lines to show where the objects go.**

I'm Mad!

Dear Jonathan,

I'm mad at you. Who says girls cannot play soccer? I can play soccer better than any boy! You know it. I defeat you every time.

The Soccer Club should not be just for boys. A club like that is not nice and not fair. I bet it was Steven's idea. I thought we were friends.

Not your best friend,
Lizzie

◆ Underline the right answers.

1. Who made Lizzie mad?

   Jonathan   Steven   her mother

2. What did Lizzie think was not fair?

   The club was Steven's idea.   The club was for boys only.

3. What does **defeat** mean?

   help   work with   beat

◆ Pretend you are Jonathan. Write a note back to Lizzie.

Dear Lizzie,

4. _____

   _____

   _____

Your friend,
Jonathan

Evan and Ken

Evan and Ken wanted to play store.
But they did not have any play money.

Evan said, "We can make our own money!"
He got paper and markers. He got out
scissors and old magazines, too.
Evan and Ken cut out some dollars.
They pasted funny magazine pictures
where the face goes. They had so
much fun, they forgot to play store.

◆ **Underline the right answers.**

1. What did Evan and Ken want to do?

   read magazines   color pictures   play store

2. What did they use for the faces on their dollars?

   magazine pictures   pictures they drew

3. What did Evan and Ken forget to do?

   play store   make play money   get scissors

◆ **Draw your own play money.**

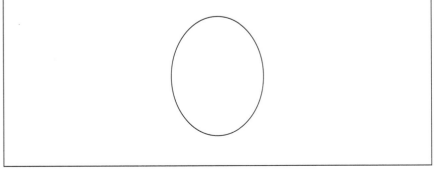

Supporting Details/Using Imagination

Dinosaur Bones

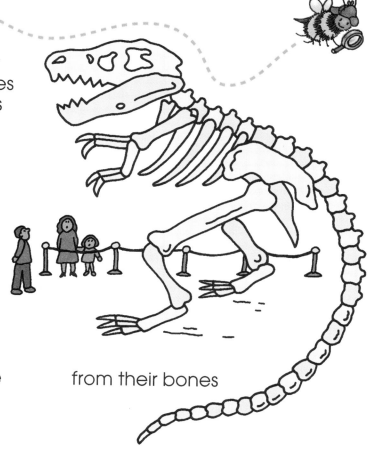

We know about dinosaurs from their bones. People hunt for dinosaur bones all over the world. They look in places where other bones were found.

Their bones can tell us how big dinosaurs were. Bones can tell us what shape they were. But bones cannot tell us what color dinosaurs were. Nobody knows that for sure.

◆ **Underline the right answers.**

1. How do we know about dinosaurs?

   from their size   from their shape   from their bones

2. What do dinosaur bones tell us?

   what size dinosaurs were   what color dinosaurs were   what dinosaurs ate

3. What don't the bones tell us?

   dinosaurs' shape   dinosaurs' size   dinosaurs' color

4. Where do people look for dinosaur bones?

   in backyards   all over the world   in the sea

5. Which dinosaur has the largest bones?

Supporting Details/Making Inferences

Will You Play?

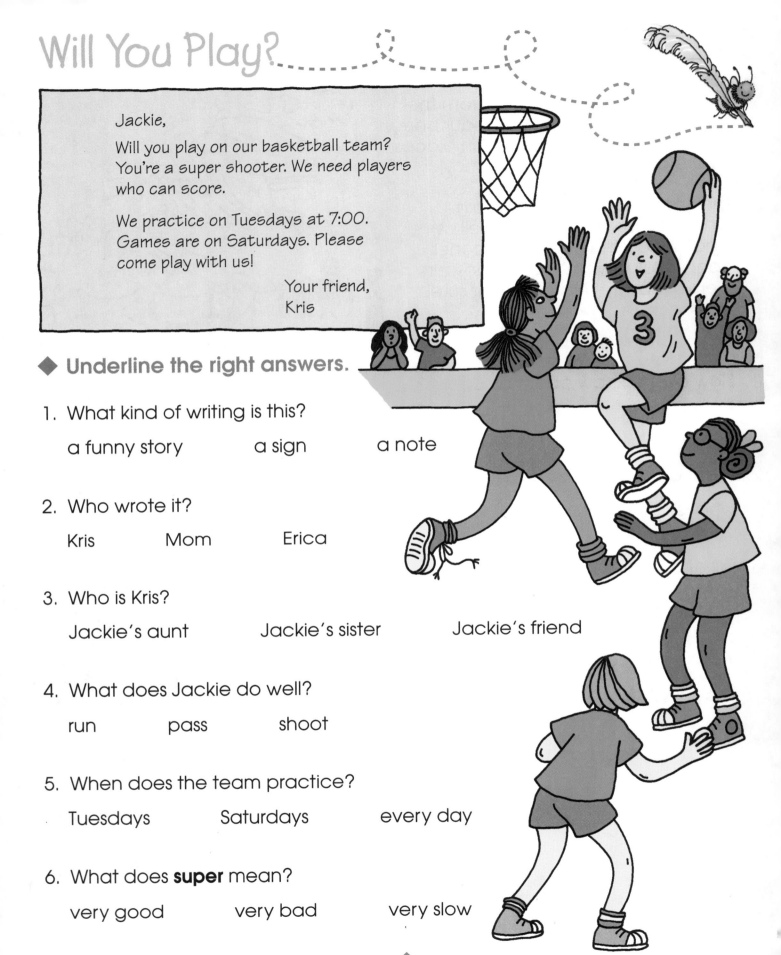

Jackie,

Will you play on our basketball team? You're a super shooter. We need players who can score.

We practice on Tuesdays at 7:00. Games are on Saturdays. Please come play with us!

Your friend,
Kris

◆ **Underline the right answers.**

1. What kind of writing is this?

   a funny story   a sign   a note

2. Who wrote it?

   Kris   Mom   Erica

3. Who is Kris?

   Jackie's aunt   Jackie's sister   Jackie's friend

4. What does Jackie do well?

   run   pass   shoot

5. When does the team practice?

   Tuesdays   Saturdays   every day

6. What does **super** mean?

   very good   very bad   very slow

Rhyming Riddles

Finish each poem with a word that rhymes.
Use these words if you need help.

white   day   snow   round   running   showers   spring

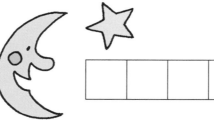

1. Clouds fly high
   when the sun is bright.
   The very best clouds
   are fluffy and _____.

2. The hot days are best
   for swimming and sunning.
   But the cool days are better
   when I want to go _____.

3. It falls from the sky
   when the cold winds blow.
   I hope it stays awhile!
   I want to play in the _____.

4. I like the flowers growing.
   I like the birds that sing.
   I like the growing season.
   We call that season _____.

5. I like sunny days
   with snow on the ground.
   And I like the nights
   when the moon is so _____.

6. April brings rain.
   May brings flowers.
   But the color in May
   makes me like April _____.

7. Some days are foggy.
   Some days are gray.
   But I like the times
   when it's sunny all _____.

Identifying Rhyming Words

A Surprise!

Paul's dad took him to the store. While they were gone, Paul's mom put up balloons. She put cups, forks, spoons, and plates on the table.

Soon, children came. They brought presents. They played and waited. Finally, Paul and his dad drove up. The children hid. When Paul came in the door, everyone yelled "Surprise!"

◆ **Underline the right answers.**

1. Which things did Paul's mom do?

   put up balloons   went to the store   set out dishes

2. Who came while Paul was gone?   his friends   his aunt

3. What did everyone say to Paul?   "Go away!"   "Surprise!"

4. What was happening at Paul's house that day?

   _____

   _____

   _____

   _____

   _____

   _____

5. Who do you think the presents were for?

   _____

   _____

Who's That?

◆ **Read the clues. Write each name under the correct picture.**

Zoe likes to spin when she skates.

Yens likes ice cream in the park.

Sue likes to skate in the park.

Joe likes to read at the beach.

Uri likes ice cream at the zoo.

Tim likes to read in his room.

1. _____

2. _____

3. _____

4. _____

5. _____

6. _____

Making Inferences/Selecting Details

In the Window...............

◆ **Look in the window. Then read each sentence. If the sentence is true, circle the letter under True. If the sentence is false, circle the letter under False.**

	True	False
1. The airplane costs $7.00.	T	G
2. The dishes cost $3.00.	O	R
3. The truck costs $8.00.	O	Y
4. Both dolls cost the same.	C	S
5. The truck costs more than the car.	T	E
6. The car costs the same as the ball.	R	O
7. The train costs the most.	R	Y
8. The ball costs the least.	E	S

◆ **Write the circled letters in the boxes.**

9. What kind of store is this?

			■				

The Brick House

The wolf was gone. The three pigs were safe together. They wanted to live in the brick house, but the house was too small.

They would add on to the house. Each pig would make a new bedroom. No pig would be lazy this time. All of the pigs would use bricks, not hay or straw. They would be ready if a wolf came again.

◆ **Underline the right answers.**

1. What is another good name for the story?

   A House for Three Pigs   Meet the Wolf!   We Can Be Lazy!

2. What was wrong with the brick house?

   It was too big.   It was too small.   It was too lazy.

3. What would the pigs do to fix it?

   make new bedrooms   make more bricks   be lazy

4. What does **lazy** mean?

   not willing to work   too silly to play   working too hard

5. Why would the pigs use bricks?

   in case a wolf came again   in case they felt lazy later

Main Idea/Supporting Details/Building Vocabulary

For Sale!

BUY MY BIKE!

Buy my spectacular bike!
It's a red and blue racer.
It has 10 speeds.

The bike is only 1 year old. It has new tires and a new chain.

I will sell my bike for $50.
I need the money to go to camp.
Call Thomas at 555-9876.

◆ Underline the right answers.

1. Is this a sign to sell a bike?   yes   no

2. Does the bike belong to Thomas?   yes   no

3. Does Thomas want you to go to camp?   yes   no

4. Does the bike have new tires?   yes   no

5. Is the bike 10 years old?   yes   no

6. Does the bike cost $50?   yes   no

7. Does **spectacular** mean "really old and ugly"?   yes   no

         Making Inferences/Supporting Details/Building Vocabulary

Giraffe Story

Giraffe likes to draw and dance. She thought she should do just one. So, Giraffe got dancing shoes. She danced every day.

Giraffe went to the tryout for the dance group. But she was too tall for the stage!

At first Giraffe was sad. Then she had a good idea! She would draw dancers. Then she would be part of both things she likes!

◆ **Underline the right answers.**

1. Did Giraffe want to be a dancer?   yes   no

2. Did Giraffe get to be a dancer?   yes   no

3. Did Giraffe go to Dancing School?   yes   no

4. What happens at a tryout?

   you find out if you can join   you find out if you are too smart

5. What is another good name for the story?

   Drawing   Dancing   Giraffe's Idea

◆ **Unscramble the words to answer the question.**

6. What was Giraffe's good idea?   dwra dcreans

   _____

   Giraffe would _____.

Supporting Details/Story Problem & Solution

Night Poem

The moon tonight
is full and bright.
The stars are shining high.

A falling star flies
before my eyes.
I make a wish as it goes by.

The darkness creeps,
but it's time to sleep.
I say "Goodnight" to the sky.

◆ **Underline the right answers.**

1. What is another good name for the poem?

   The Sun   Goodnight Sky   Darkness

2. What is not named in the poem?

   the stars   the sun   a falling star

3. Which word rhymes with **tonight**?

   high   sky   bright

4. What is full and bright?

   the moon   the stars   darkness

◆ **Underline the missing words.**

5. _____ means "move slowly."   **Creep**   **Bright**

6. _____ means "go through the air."   **Sleep**   **Fly**

Main Idea/Rhyming Words/Building Vocabulary

Write a Letter

The United States has a president. Grownups vote for the president. The president works for all of us.

What would you like to tell the president? Write a letter to him. Here is his address.

The President
The White House
1600 Pennsylvania Avenue
Washington, D.C. 20500

◆ Write a letter to the president.

Date: _____

Dear Mr. President,

_____

My name is _____ . I think

_____
_____
_____
_____
_____
_____

Your friend,

_____
_____

Think Up an Invention

Once there were no TVs. Once there were no cars or telephones. People invented these things.

Think of something that you would like to have. Make your invention something people have never seen.

◆ **Answer the questions.**
Draw a picture of your invention.

1. What are three things that were invented?

_____

_ _ _ _ _ _ _ _ _ _ _ _ _ _ _ _ _ _

_____

_ _ _ _ _ _ _ _ _ _ _ _ _ _ _ _ _ _

_____

_____

_ _ _ _ _ _ _ _ _ _ _ _ _ _ _ _ _ _

_____

2. What is the name of your invention?

_____

_ _ _ _ _ _ _ _ _ _ _ _ _ _ _ _ _ _

_____

3. What will your invention do?

_____

_ _ _ _ _ _ _ _ _ _ _ _ _ _ _ _ _ _

_____

My Invention

_ _

_____

_ _

_____

Native Americans

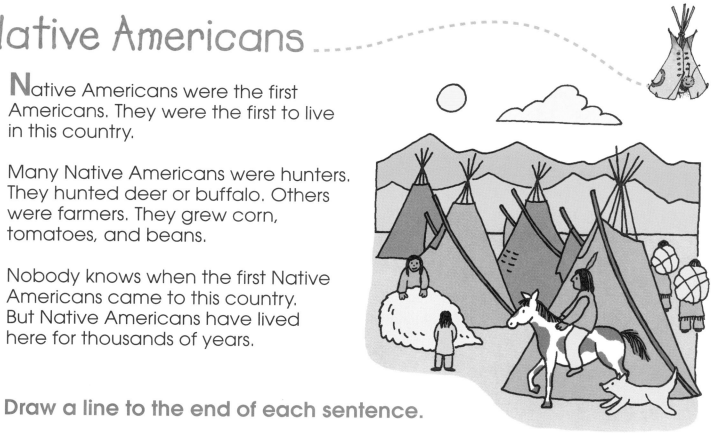

Native Americans were the first Americans. They were the first to live in this country.

Many Native Americans were hunters. They hunted deer or buffalo. Others were farmers. They grew corn, tomatoes, and beans.

Nobody knows when the first Native Americans came to this country. But Native Americans have lived here for thousands of years.

◆ **Draw a line to the end of each sentence.**

1. Native Americans were the

2. Nobody knows when the first

3. Many Native Americans

Native Americans came to this country.

were hunters.

first Americans.

◆ **Underline the right answers.**

4. What did some Native Americans hunt?

5. What did some Native Americans grow?

Cooking

Kids can cook. Some kids cook French toast for breakfast. Some kids cook tacos for dinner. Lots of kids cook soup for lunch.

How do kids learn to cook? They learn from their parents. They read about cooking in books.

All good cooks are careful. Kid cooks should not cook without a grownup to help.

◆ **Underline the right answers.**

1. What is another good name for the story?

   Kid Cooks   Cook Books   How to Cook

2. What foods can some kids cook?

   French toast   tacos   soup   cake

3. What is one way kids learn?

   from their parents   from younger kids   by thinking

4. How are all good cooks the same?

   They all play in the kitchen.   They are all careful.

◆ **Write your answer on the line.**

_____

_ _ _ _ _ _ _ _ _ _ _ _ _ _ _ _ _ _ _

5. What do you like to cook? _____

Where Do Things Go?

At Sol's house, the bedrooms are upstairs.

At Sol's house, the kitchen is downstairs.

At Sol's house, the bathroom is upstairs.

At Sol's house, the living room is downstairs.

At Sol's house, the baby's room is upstairs.

At Sol's house, the hallway is downstairs.

◆ Unscramble the words. Draw a line from each word to a room in Sol's house. Use these words if you need help.

beds   couch   stove   stairs   crib   bathtub

1. bdse _____

_ _ _ _ _ _ _ _ _ _ _

_____

2. vetso _____

_ _ _ _ _ _ _ _ _ _ _

_____

3. ribc _____

_ _ _ _ _ _ _ _ _ _ _

_____

4. bhatbtu _____

_ _ _ _ _ _ _ _ _ _ _

_____

5. ochuc _____

_ _ _ _ _ _ _ _ _ _ _

_____

6. tasirs _____

_ _ _ _ _ _ _ _ _ _ _

_____

Make a Bank

Is there something you want to buy? Save your money! Make a bank. All you need is a plastic milk bottle, markers, and some tape.

Clean the milk bottle. Tape on the cap to keep your money safe. Have a grownup help cut a slot for the money. Draw pictures on the bank. Then drop your money inside.

1. What do you need to make a bank?

new shoes	milk bottle	apples
some tape	a grownup	markers

◆ Put the steps in order. Write **1, 2, 3, 4, 5,** and **6.**

2. ☐ Drop your money in.   ☐ Get a milk bottle.   ☐ Draw pictures.

☐ Clean the bottle.   ☐ Tape on the cap.   ☐ Cut a slot.

Selecting Details/Steps in a Process

Pink Day!

When Kim went outside, the world had changed. Everything was pink! The sky was pink. The houses were pink. Even the grass was pink. Pink children were playing on pink sidewalks. Pink cars were driving on pink streets.

Kim did not like what she saw. Then Kim remembered. She had on her pink sunglasses. She took them off, and the world returned to normal.

◆ **Underline the right answers.**

1. What is another good name for the story?

   Pink Shoes   Kim Sees Pink   Kim Goes Walking

2. What was the problem?

   Everything was pink.   Kim went outside.

3. What did Kim do to make the world look okay?

   She went back outside.   She took off her sunglasses.

4. What does **normal** mean?

   the way things usually are   a strange and new way

Jump Rope Chant

Flowers in the garden.
Flowers by the walk.
Flowers in the forest.
I wish they could talk.

Flowers dancing in the wind
and sprouting up in May.
If I met a flower friend,
what would I have to say?

◆ **Underline the right answers.**

1. What kind of writing is this?

   a letter   a story   a poem

2. What do flowers do in the wind?

   grow   dance   talk

3. What does **sprouting up** mean?

   getting planted   starting to grow

◆ **Draw a line to each word that rhymes.**

4. walk   shower

   May   talk

   flower   say

   wish   fish

Things That Move

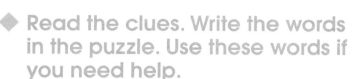

◆ Read the clues. Write the words in the puzzle. Use these words if you need help.

airplane   boat   bus   car   skates   train   truck

Across ▶

1. This goes on water.

4. This can have 2 doors or 4.

6. This goes through the air.

Down ▼

1. This goes to school.

2. This goes on tracks.

3. These go on your feet.

5. This is bigger than a car.

How Many?

1. Two kids got on the bus. The bus stopped later. Three more kids got on. How many kids were on the bus?

2. Five presents were on the table. Henry opened two of them. How many presents were left?

3. Mike went to the library. He picked 3 funny books. He picked 1 scary book. How many books did Mike pick?

4. Jan had a calendar. She colored one box on Monday. She colored one box on Tuesday and one on Wednesday. How many boxes were colored?

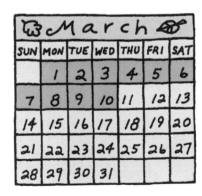

Selecting Details/Making Inferences

In the Sky!

Sky Boy could fly. He lived in the sky. He used clouds for his bed and played tag with the birds.

Sky Boy could slide down rays of the sun. He could ride on the wind like a kite. He took showers in the rain and rode around on tornadoes.

Sky Boy had one job. He painted the rainbows after it rained. That was more fun than all of his games.

◆ **Underline the right answers.**

1. What is another good name for the story?

   Rainbows   Sky Boy   Playing in the Rain

2. Can Sky Boy fly?   yes   no

3. Can Sky Boy paint?   yes   no

4. Can Sky Boy make it rain?   yes   no

5. Does Sky Boy play with birds?   yes   no

6. Does Sky Boy play slide in the rain?   yes   no

◆ **Unscramble the words to answer the question.**

7. What was Sky Boy's favorite thing to do?   tnpai a rbaoinw

   _____

   _

   _____

In an Emergency....

If you have an emergency, ask a grownup to help. If you cannot find a grownup, call 911. People at 911 will help you be safe. They will help you fix what is wrong.

When 911 answers, tell that person your name. Tell where you live and what is wrong. Then listen carefully. The 911 person will tell you what to do next.

Never call 911 if nothing is wrong. People at 911 are busy helping callers who need help right away.

◆ **Underline the right answers.**

1. What is another good name for the story?

   Calling Mom   Call 911   Telephone Games

2. What should you **never** do?

   call 911 when nothing is wrong   look for a grownup

3. What does **emergency** mean?

   a happy time at home   a dangerous problem that needs help quickly

◆ **Write 1, 2, 3, and 4 to show the right order.**

4. _____ Listen carefully for what you should do next.

   _____ Call 911.

   _____ Try to find a grownup.

   _____ Tell your name, where you live, and what is wrong.

Ben's Robot

Ben had a robot
who never forgot
anything Ben ever told him.

Sometimes the robot would do
what Ben told him not to.
Then Ben would quietly scold him.

◆ Underline the right answers.

1. What is another good name for the poem?

   Robot Thinks   Bad Ben!   The Robot Forgets

2. What does the robot never do?

   forget   anything   talk

3. What does the robot never forget?

   what he sees   what Ben tells him

4. What does **scold** mean?

   to say you did something wrong   to say you did something right

◆ Draw a line to each word that rhymes.

5. told   forgot

   robot   to

   do   scold

The Award

The city gave an award today. The award is for the school that reads the most books. Lincoln School won.

The children at Lincoln School will pick out new books. The books go in the school library. Now the children can keep on reading.

◆ **Underline the right answers.**

1. Where is this writing?

   in a birthday card   in a note to school   in a newspaper

2. What is another good name for the story?

   Lincoln School Wins   The City Is Nice   Awards Are Good

3. What did the children at Lincoln School do?

   read the most books   made art   wrote stories

4. What does **award** mean?

   a book   a day off   a prize

◆ **Write the title of a book you read. Write what the story was about.**

_____

_____

5. _____

_____

_____

Follow the Map

Nina's club is going somewhere. It's a surprise. The club leader gave the kids directions. She gave them a map. The kids meet at the clubhouse to start. Where are the kids going?

◆ **Start at the clubhouse. Draw a line to mark where the kids go.**

1. Leave the clubhouse.
   Go left on Cent Street.

2. Walk down Cent Street to Ash Street.
   Turn right on Ash Street.

3. Walk by the hot dog stand.

4. Turn right on Main Street.

5. Walk to the red house.
   Then look across Main Street.
   What store do you see?

Main Street

Ash Street   Elm Street   Oak Street   May Street

First Street

Cent Street

The surprise store is _____ .

Following Directions

A Scary House!

Maria, Ted, and Sara liked to pretend they were ghost finders. But they never went near the scary house. Everyone said that a ghost lived in the scary house. Everyone said, "Don't go there!"

One day the kids went to the house. They walked slowly. They were afraid. They rang the bell. Slowly the door opened.

◆ **What could happen next?**
Write how the story ends.

_____

_____

_____ was at the door. The

_____

_____ said to them,

"_____"

_____

_____

"_____

_____

The kids answered, _____

_____"

_____

_____

Then all of a sudden, _____,

_____

_____

and the kids ran. Maria, Ted, and Sara _____

_____

_____

Answer Key

Page 1
1. I'm the Best Me!
2. wiggle
3. really great
4. buzz

Page 2
1. bridge
3. stems
5. A's
2. glass
4. wheels
6. trapeze ropes

Page 3
1. My Bones Are Missing!
2. think
3. Dog used them.
4. not think about what you do
5. bone picture

Page 4
1. **any two:**
   paper crayons
   pencil stapler

2. 2   1   3
   5   4

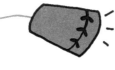

Page 5
1st mouse played a drum
2nd mouse hummed along
3rd mouse danced around
4th mouse clapped his hands
5th mouse sang a song

Page 6
1. picture 2
2. picture 2
3. picture 2
4. picture 1

Page 7
Across
1. shaker
3. shovel
5. path
6. hose
7. ear

Down
2. rake
3. shoe
4. vase

	s	h	a	k	e	r	
						a	
						k	
			s	h	o	v	e	l
p	a	t	h			a	
			o			s	
h	o	s	e			e	a	r

Page 8
1. No T
2. No H
3. Yes E
4. Yes R
5. Yes A
6. Yes I
7. No N

8. THE RAIN

Page 9
1. a cat who uses a computer
2. yes
3. no
4. yes
5. cat at computer

Page 10
1. Henry's Dream
2. a lion chasing him
3. in the jungle
4. a bad dream
5. was red.
   were always white.
   woke up.

Page 11
Answers will vary, but should include names and descriptions.

Page 12
1. families
2. baths
3. day
4. 200

Page 13
1. an ad
2. at a pet store
3. dog shampoo
4. very quickly
5. dog baths

Page 14
1. Snake Soup
2. noodle soup
3. to scoop
4. snakes
5. Grandma

Page 15
Lines show paper things going to the paper bin.
Lines show plastic things going to the plastic bin.
Lines show cans going to the can bin.

Page 16
1. book fair
2. books
3. books
4. gym
5. all day
6. Answers will vary.

Answer Key

Answer Key

Page 17
1. a note
2. next week
3. maple, oak, elm
4. keep it green
5. picture of people planting trees

Page 18
1. shoe picture
2. chose the one you wanted
3. baseball

   Answers will vary.

Page 19
1. a sign
2. to find a lost dog
3. something given for doing a good deed
4. black dog with a white face and tail

Page 20
1. sound
2. early morning
3. bed
4. mice picture

Page 21
two zebras
one elephant
ten snakes
one giraffe
four monkeys

Page 22
1. a flashlight and some friends
2. 3   1   2
   5   4   6

Page 23
1. Real Working Animals
   Where Real Trains Go
   A Ride Long Ago
   Silly Animal Stories
2. 1, 2, 3
3. 4
4. Answers will vary.

Page 24
Things People Play
drum   guitar
horn   violin

Things People Wear
shirt   shoes
hat   socks

Things People Eat
pizza   chili
salad   tacos

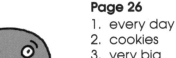

Page 25
1. Make a Telephone
2. a telephone
3. in the bottom of both cups
4. in both ends of the string
5. Answers will vary.

Page 26
1. every day
2. cookies
3. very big
4. door
5. please

Page 27
1. snake picture
2. under the sink
3. broom picture
4. The snake was just a toy.

Page 28
1. to the circus
2. laugh
3. Sunday, June 9 at 3:00
4. someone who puts on a show

Page 29
Answers will vary.

Page 30
Across
3. horse
4. bear
7. elephant
8. panda
9. snake
Down
1. monkey
2. zebra
5. anteater
6. seal

Page 31
1. picture 2
2. picture 1
3. picture 1
4. picture 2

Page 32
Left side:
watering can, hose and sprinkler
Back wall:
shovel, spade
Outside on the right:
lawn mowers

Answer Key

Answer Key

Page 33
1. Jonathan
2. The club was for boys only.
3. beat
4. Answers will vary.

Page 34
1. play store
2. magazine pictures
3. play store

Pictures will vary.

Page 35
1. from their bones
2. what size dinosaurs were
3. dinosaurs' color
4. all over the world
5. middle dinosaur

Page 36
1. a note
2. Kris
3. Jackie's friend
4. shoot
5. Tuesdays
6. very good

Page 37
1. white
2. running
3. snow
4. spring
5. round
6. showers
7. day

Page 38
1. put up balloons set out dishes
2. his friends
3. "Surprise!"
4. He was having a surprise birthday party.
5. Paul

Page 39
1. Sue   2. Uri   3. Joe
4. Tim   5. Yens 6. Zoe

Page 40
1. true T
2. true O
3. false Y
4. false S
5. true T
6. false O
7. true R
8. true E

9. TOY STORE

Page 41
1. A House for Three Pigs
2. It was too small.
3. make new bedrooms
4. not willing to work
5. in case a wolf came again

Page 42
1. yes
2. yes
3. no
4. yes
5. no
6. yes
7. no

Page 43
1. yes
2. no
3. no
4. you find out if you can join
5. Giraffe's Idea
6. draw dancers.

Page 44
1. Goodnight Sky
2. the sun
3. bright
4. the moon
5. Creep
6. Fly

Page 45
Answers will vary, but should include date, name, message, and signature.

Page 46
1. TVs cars telephones
2. Names will vary.
3. Descriptions will vary.

Page 47
1. first Americans.
2. Native Americans came to this country.
3. were hunters.
4. buffalo picture
5. corn picture

Page 48
1. Kid Cooks
2. French toast, tacos, soup
3. from their parents
4. They are all careful.
5. Answers will vary.

Page 49
1. beds (bedroom)
2. stove (kitchen)
3. crib (baby's room)
4. bathtub (bathroom)
5. couch (living room)
6. stairs (hallway)

Answer Key

Page 50
1. milk bottle
   markers
   some tape
   a grownup

2. 6   l   5
   2   3   4

Page 51
1. Kim Sees Pink
2. Everything was pink.
3. She took off her sunglasses.
4. the way things usually are

Page 52
1. a poem
2. dance
3. starting to grow
4. talk
   say
   shower
   fish

Page 53

Across
1. boat
4. car
6. airplane

Down
1. bus
2. train
3. skates
5. truck

Page 54
1. picture 2
2. picture 2
3. picture 1
4. picture 2

Page 55
1. Sky Boy
2. yes
3. yes
4. no
5. yes
6. no
7. paint a rainbow

```
[1]b o a [2]t
     u      r
[3]  s  [4]c a r
  k  [5]t      i
[6]a i r p l a n e
  t      u
  e      c
  s      k
```

Page 56
1. Call 911
2. call 911 when nothing is wrong
3. a dangerous problem that needs help quickly

4. 4
   2
   1
   3

Page 57
1. Bad Ben!
2. forget
3. what Ben tells him
4. to say you did something wrong
5. scold
   forgot
   to

Page 58
1. in a newspaper
2. Lincoln School Wins
3. read the most books
4. a prize
5. Answers will vary.

Page 59
Line on the map should go left from the clubhouse down Cent Street to Ash Street. Right past a hot dog stand. Right on Main Street to a red house. Look across Main Street to see the ice cream store.

the ice cream store.

Page 60
Answers will vary, but should tell a story.

   64   Reading Comprehension, Grade 2 **02242**